YOUNG ADULT

The ELI Readers collection is a complete range of books and plays for readers of all ages, ranging from captivating contemporary stories to timeless classics. There are three series, each catering for a different age group; Young ELI Readers, Teen ELI Readers and Young Adult ELI Readers. The books are carefully edited and beautifully illustrated to capture the essence of the stories and plots.

The readers are supplemented with 'Focus on' texts packed with background cultural information about the writers and their lives and times.

The FSC certification guarantees that the paper used in these publications comes from certified forests, promoting responsible forestry management worldwide.

For this series of ELI graded readers, we have planted 5000 new trees.

Sir Arthur Conan Doyle

A Study in Scarlet

Adaptation and Activities by Elizabeth Ferretti
Illustrated by Riccardo Guasco

YOUNG ADULT ELI READERS

A Study in Scarlet
Sir Arthur Conan Doyle
Adaptation and Activities by Elizabeth Ferretti
Language Level Consultant: Lisa Suett
Illustrated by Riccardo Guasco

ELI Readers
Founder and Series Editors
Paola Accattoli, Grazia Ancillani, Daniele Garbuglia (Art Director)

Graphic Design
Airone Comunicazione - Sergio Elisei

Layout
Airone Comunicazione

Production Manager
Francesco Capitano

Photo credits
Shutterstock, ELI Archive

© 2016 ELI s.r.l.
P.O. Box 6
62019 Recanati MC
Italy
T +39 071750701
F +39 071977851
info@elionline.com
www.elionline.com

Printed in Italy by Tecnostampa Recanati – ERA114.01
ISBN 978-88-536-2107-8

First edition: March 2016

www.elireaders.com

Contents

6	Main Characters	
8	Activities	
10	Chapter 1	**Mr Sherlock Holmes**
18	Activities	
20	Chapter 2	**The Lauriston Gardens Mystery**
28	Activities	
30	Chapter 3	**The Wrong Man**
38	Activities	
40	Chapter 4	**Lucy Ferrier**
48	Activities	
50	Chapter 5	**The End of the Game**
56	Activities	
58	Focus on...	**A Study in Scarlet**
59	Focus on...	**Sir Arthur Conan Doyle**
60	Focus on...	**The Sherlock Holmes Museum**
61	Focus on...	*Sherlock*
62	Test	
63	Syllabus	

These icons indicate the parts of the story that are recorded

start ▶ stop ■

MAIN CHARACTERS

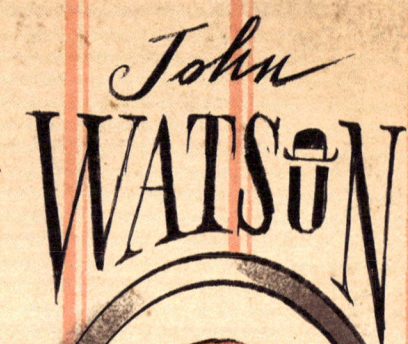

John WATSON

Sherlock HOLMES

Lestrade

Lucy FERRIER.

Jefferson HOPE

Drebber

PRE-READING ACTIVITIES

Vocabulary

1 Find the right word from the box.

> cheap • doctor • expensive • finish • forget •
> hospital • remember • start

1 This person helps you when you're not well. _____.
2 He/She often works in a _____.
3 When you pay a lot of money for something, it's _____.
4 When you don't pay much for something, it's _____.
5 When you think of something again, you _____ it.
6 When you don't think of something again, you _____ it.
7 When you leave university, you _____ studying.
8 When you go to university for the first time, you _____ studying.

Grammar

2 Find the right word from the box.

> after • before • so • when

1 _____ I came to London, I was in Afghanistan for two years.
2 _____ I was well again, I came to London by boat.
3 I had no friends in London, _____ I didn't have anyone to talk to.
4 _____ walking for five minutes, I heard someone say my name.

Comprehension

3 Read these sentences, then tick True or False below.

'Dr Watson is looking for somewhere to live,' Stamford said.

Sherlock looked happy when he heard that. 'I've found a nice place in Baker Street,' he said, 'I think you'll like it, but will you like me?'

'I think so,' I answered.

'Sometimes I don't speak for many days,' he said, 'and I play music. Will that be a problem?'

'I don't talk much,' I said, 'and I like music when it's played well.'

		T	F
1	Dr Watson needs a new home.	☐	☐
2	Sherlock Holmes has found a home in Baker Street.	☐	☐
3	Sherlock Holmes says that Dr Watson will like him.	☐	☐
4	Sherlock Holmes and Dr Watson like making a lot of noise.	☐	☐

Listening

▶ 3 **4** Who said this? Listen and find out.

> Sherlock Holmes • Stamford • Dr Watson

1 Where did you go... Watson? _____
2 Do you know anyone who can help me? _____
3 That's good! _____
4 'I have it! I have it!' _____
5 How did you know that? _____

Chapter 1

Mr Sherlock Holmes

▶ 2 My name is Dr John Watson. It's 1881 and I'm living in a hotel in London, but for two years before this, I was in Afghanistan. There were problems between the British and the Afghans then. I'm a doctor and I went there because they needed my help. After some months I felt very bad and I had to stay in hospital in India for a long time. When I was better, I came to London by boat.

I don't have a house in England, so when I arrived I went to live in a hotel in a good street in London. Everyone goes to London, it's an exciting city! My hotel is nice and clean but life isn't easy. I'm not a well man and, because I don't have any friends or family here, I don't have anyone to talk to. My biggest problem is the hotel, it's too expensive. Yesterday, I started to look for somewhere cheaper to live.

***

▶ 3 This morning I needed to think, so I went for a walk. After a few minutes, I heard someone say my name. I looked behind me and saw an old friend called Stamford, who studied with me to be a doctor. We went to have lunch.

10

'Where did you go after you finished university, Watson?' he asked, when we got to the restaurant. 'You don't look well, but your face is brown!'

I told him about Afghanistan and India.

'Now, I'm looking for somewhere to live. Do you know anyone who can help me?' I said, when I finished.

'Yes, Sherlock Holmes,' Stamford said. 'He often comes to the hospital where I work. He's looking for someone to live with him.'

'That's good!' I said, happily.

Stamford looked at me. 'You don't know Sherlock Holmes, do you? He's not a bad man, but he can be… difficult.'

We arrived at London Hospital and went into a big room. There was only one student working there.

When he saw us, he said excitedly, 'I have it! I have it!'

'Dr Watson, this is Sherlock Holmes,' said Stamford.

'How are you ?' Sherlock Holmes said to me. He looked friendly. 'I see that you were in Afghanistan before you came to London.'

'How did you know that?' I asked.

▶ 4   'It's not important,' he said. 'Today, I found something that will help the police*!'

'Help the police?'

Sherlock Holmes didn't answer my question.

'Dr Watson is looking for somewhere to live,' Stamford said.

'That's good,' he said, 'tomorrow I'm going to look at a nice place in Baker Street. It's very nice. There is a woman who will cook and clean for us. I think you'll like it, but will you like me?'

'I think so,' I answered.

---

police the police help us be safe; they catch bad people

11

'Sometimes I don't speak for many days,' he said, 'and I play the violin*. Will that be a problem?'

'I don't talk much,' I said, 'and I like the violin when it's played well.'

'Then meet me here tomorrow at twelve o'clock,' he said. 'Goodbye!' and he went back to his work. We left him.

'How did he know I was in Afghanistan? Did you tell him?' I asked Stamford.

'No,' said Stamford, 'that's Sherlock Holmes! He knows everything, and nobody understands how. It's a mystery*!'

I thought about my new friend that night, and the next day we went together to 221B Baker Street.

The rooms were good and not expensive. There were two bedrooms and a big living room with two windows. That evening I moved my things from the hotel.

Sherlock Holmes isn't a difficult man to live with. He doesn't talk much, he goes to bed before ten, has an early breakfast and often goes to the hospital to work.

Sherlock Holmes is very tall and thin and has a long nose like a bird. When he looks at me, I always feel he can hear what I'm thinking! I watch him every day, but I can't understand much about him or the work he does. He's a mystery!

★★★

I often got up from bed late, but one morning I woke up early and went into the living room. It was 4th March, I remember the day well,

---

violin

mystery something that is difficult to understand

1

because this was when everything started! Sherlock Holmes was at breakfast. I said good morning, sat down at the table with him and started to read the newspaper. Then I saw something that looked interesting. It was called "The Book of Life" and I started to read.

> *It is important to look. You can learn a lot from looking hard and thinking about what you see. For example, you can learn everything about a man by looking at his face and watching how he walks or talks. You can understand what he is thinking and you will know what he did yesterday, and what he will do tomorrow. You could think this is not possible, but I know that it is possible. Give me a small cup of water and I can tell you if it is from the Atlantic or the Niagara. If you work hard you will be great.*
> *You must start with easy questions. When you meet someone for the first time, you can learn, with only one short look, what his job is. Look at his hands, look at his clothes, his shirt and his boots. Put all of this together, then you will have your answer.*
> *If you do this, then you will understand every mystery!*

'Are you studying to be a doctor?' I asked, after I put butter on my bread.

He looked at me with *those* eyes. 'No,' he answered.

Next, I asked him about some famous writers, and what he thought about their books. He didn't know any of them.

Then I asked him about the world. 'Do you know that our world goes around the sun?' I said.

'No, I don't' he said. 'And now, I will forget what you said!'

'Forget that our world goes around the sun?' I asked.

'Yes, that is what I said. You see, it's not good to remember too much,' he said, 'I think that our heads are like a small house. You cannot put hundreds of tables and chairs inside. If you bring a new chair in, then you have to take one out. I only remember things that are important.'

'But…' I said.

'To know that our world goes around the sun isn't important for my work,' he said. 'I look at everything, I watch everyone and I ask many questions about what I see. I work hard to understand things that other people can't understand. It's my business, it's how I pay for my bread and cheese.'

'How?' I asked.

'Here in London we have a lot of policemen,' he said, 'but they're not very good policemen. They, and other people, come to ask my help. They pay me to find answers to their questions.'

'I see,' I said. I thought for a minute, then I asked, 'How did you know I was in Afghanistan?'

'You are not a well man and your face and hands are brown, but your arms are white. I think you were in a hot country. The British have problems in Afghanistan, so it's easy! That's where you were before you came to London.'

'Ah!' I said. 'Stamford said you always know everything.'

'I think a lot,' he said 'That's why I'm different from most people!'

Every week people came to see him. They often looked sad, some of them seemed to have a lot of problems. Once it was a young girl, then an old woman came and talked to him for a long time. Another day it was an old man who looked very poor. One man, Mr Lestrade, visited us many times. When these people came, I went to my bedroom.

Sherlock said he couldn't talk to me about what they told him. When they left they sometimes looked happy, and sometimes they looked sadder than when they arrived. Mr Lestrade always walked away very quickly when he left us.

★★★

This was our life for many months. In that time I started to feel better. I liked living in Baker Street, I liked Sherlock. Then one morning Sherlock wasn't happy. He took his violin and started to play, but stopped after two minutes.

'It's so boring today,' he said. 'There's nothing exciting in this city. I'm the best man in London to help the police, but I can't help them if they don't come to me!'

I looked out of the window and saw a man walking on Baker Street, looking at all the numbers on the doors. He saw our door, 221B, and ran across the road to our house. The woman who lives at the bottom of the house opened the door. The man came up to our rooms.

'For Mr Sherlock Holmes,' he said. He gave my friend a letter, then he left.

'Ah,' said Sherlock Holmes. 'Now, this is more interesting!'

2

AFTER-READING ACTIVITIES

Comprehension

1 Answer the questions.

1 Where is Dr Watson living when we first meet him?

2 Where do Dr Watson and Stamford go after they meet in the park?

3 Which hospital do they find Sherlock Holmes in?

4 What things does Sherlock say that he doesn't do?

5 Sherlock says to Watson that he has a hobby. What is it?

6 Why does Sherlock say he will forget that the world goes around the sun?

7 How does Sherlock know that Watson was in Afghanistan?

8 How is Sherlock feeling when the young man brings the letter?

2 Who is it?

1 This person doesn't have much money. He's looking for a new place to live. He studied to be a doctor. He doesn't have many friends. _____

2 This person has found a place to live. He gets excited about things. He's friendly. He studies a lot. He's a mystery. _____

3 This person studied to be a doctor. He works at London Hospital. He has a friend who's looking for someone to live with. _____

Grammar

3 Use 'some + one/thing/where' or 'any + one/thing' to finish these sentences.

1 I'm looking for ___somewhere___ cheaper to live.
2 I heard _____ say my name.
3 Do you know _____ who can help me?
4 I found _____ that will help the police.
5 I watched him, but I couldn't understand _____ about him.

PRE-READING ACTIVITY

Writing

4 What do you think is in the letter?

Chapter 2

The Lauriston Gardens Mystery

▶ 5 'Will you read it to me?' Sherlock asked, giving me the letter.

'My dear Mr Sherlock Holmes,' I read. 'Last night, we found the body of a man at 3 Lauriston Gardens in Brixton, London. A policeman saw a light in a house where no one is living now and went to look. Inside he found a dead* man. He had a lot of business cards with the name *Enoch J. Drebber*, *Cleveland*, *Ohio*, *USA* on them. We cannot understand how he died, and no one took his money or his watch. It's a mystery. Lestrade is also here. Will you come to the house and help us?

Yours, Tobias Gregson.'

'I'll get a taxi!' I said.

'Those two policemen, Gregson and Lestrade, won't tell anyone if I help them, but I think it'll be fun to find an answer to this mystery, don't you? Come on!'

We got our hats and coats and one minute later we were in a taxi going to Lauriston Gardens. On our journey Sherlock didn't say anything about the dead man, he only talked about violins!

The taxi arrived in Brixton and we got out. Number 3 Lauriston Gardens wasn't a nice house. The windows were dark and cold, in the garden the plants were tall and big.

dead not living

Sherlock didn't go in to the house, but stayed outside, looking at the road and the garden for a long time. I couldn't understand what he was doing. The dead man was in the house not in the garden or on the road! Then, after ten or fifteen minutes, we went to the door where we met a tall man with blonde hair. He had a book and pencil in his hand.

'Good morning, Mr Gregson,' said Sherlock.

'Good morning Mr Holmes. I am happy you're here!' Gregson answered. 'Lestrade is inside. Come with me.'

I followed them into the hall. On the right was an open door, but I didn't want to see what was in the room! It was a big room, but there were no tables or chairs in it. The only thing in the room was the dead man. He was about forty-three or forty-four years old and had expensive clothes on. I looked at his face. He looked like a bad man and I thought the world was better now he was dead! But we had to find out why he died. Most importantly, we had to find out who did it.

Sherlock went to the dead man and looked at him, his clothes and the room. There was a lot of blood* on the floor, but it was not from the dead man. He didn't have any blood on his body.

After twenty minutes, Sherlock finished. Four policemen came in and picked the dead man up and, under him, there was a small ring* on the floor.

'Did the man have anything inside his coat?' asked Sherlock Holmes.

'Yes,' answered Gregson, taking out his book. 'I wrote it down. He had a large ring, some business cards with the name *Enoch J. Drebber*, a book with the name Joseph Stangerson written inside, and two letters about a boat to New York that Drebber and Stangerson wanted to take.'

---

blood red 'water' in your body   **ring**

'Does anyone know Stangerson?' asked Sherlock.

'I sent a message to Cleveland in the USA this morning,' said Gregson, 'but we've heard nothing from them.'

Lestrade was at the back of the room. 'Look!' he said, 'There's writing on the wall!'

We went over and saw the word 'RACHE' written in blood!

'It's a woman's name – Rachel,' said Lestrade. 'The person who wrote this didn't finish. This is all about a woman!'

'No!' said Sherlock. 'There is no Rachel here! Rache is the German word for 'revenge'. I think Drebber is dead because he did something bad to the man who wrote 'Rache', and now that man wanted to do something bad to Drebber – that is revenge! Now,' Sherlock said, 'we must speak to the policeman who found the body last night. What is his name and where does he live?'

'He's called John Rance,' Lestrade said, 'He's a good man but he won't be pleased to see you. He was working last night and now he is sleeping.'

Sherlock wasn't listening to that!

'Where does he live?' he asked again.

'You will find him at 46 Audley Court, Kennington Park Gate. It's not far,' said Gregson.

'Thank you,' said Sherlock, 'We will only speak to him for a short time. Then he can go back to sleep. I think a dead man is more important than a few minutes of sleep, don't you?'

We left Lestrade and Gregson. Outside in the street we found a taxi. We jumped in and told the driver to take us to a street not far away.

'I think that Drebber and another man arrived in a taxi,' said Sherlock while we were travelling to see Mr Rance, who was at this

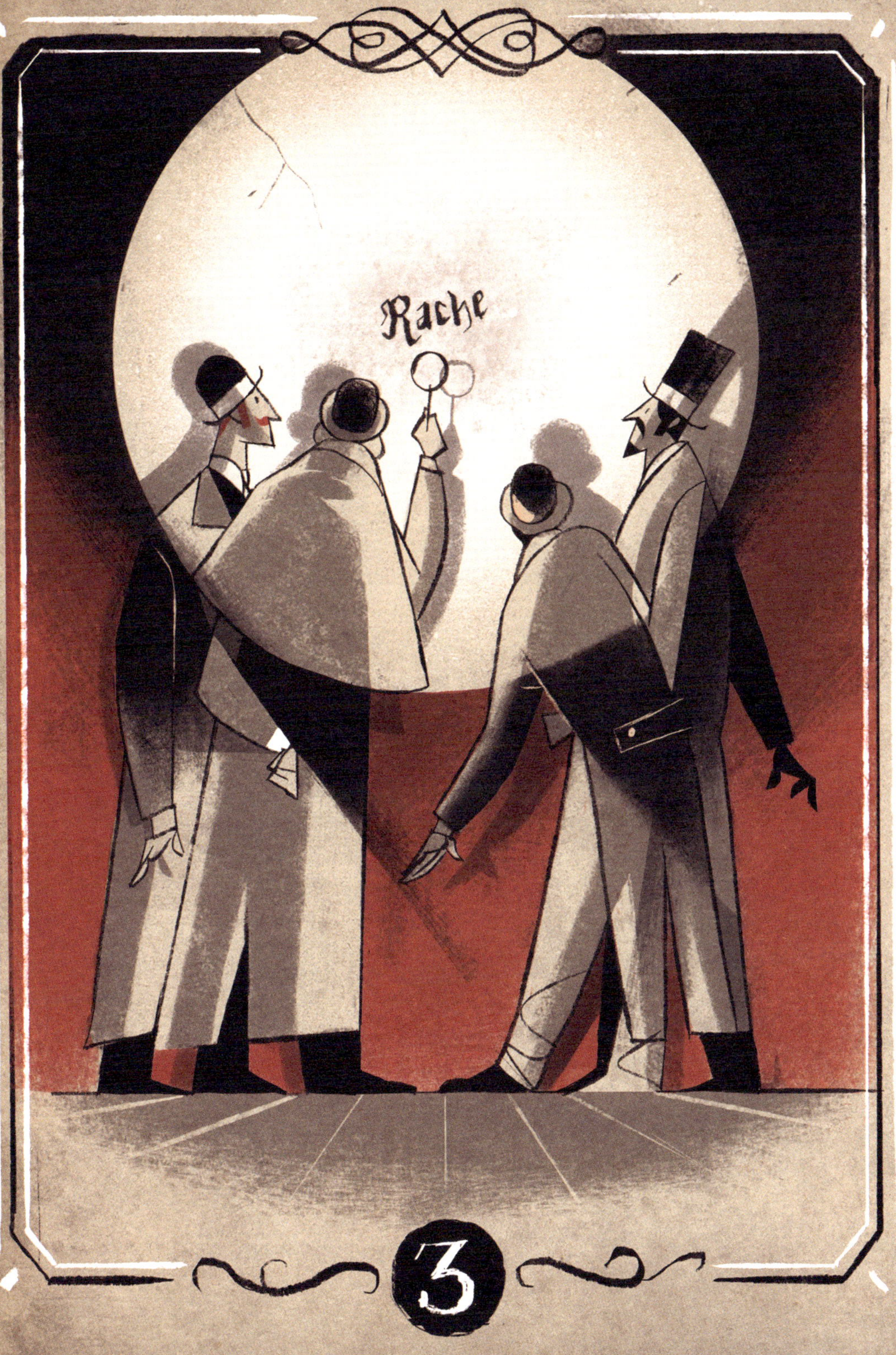
Rache
3

time asleep in his bed. He didn't know we were coming to wake him up! 'He gave Drebber something very bad to eat – a poison*. That's how he died. The other man is tall.'

'Where's the taxi driver?' I asked. 'Where did the blood come from? Why did the tall man want Drebber to die? Why did Drebber eat the poison? Why did the tall man write RACHE?'

'It's difficult,' said Sherlock. 'I think we'll call this mystery 'A Study in Scarlet*', because scarlet is the colour of blood!'

Sherlock and I went to knock at the door of the policeman who found Drebber's body. His wife opened the door and kindly called her husband for us. When he came out of his bedroom, he looked very tired and I felt sad for him. Sherlock didn't see that, he just started asking about what happened in Lauriston Gardens.

'It was two in the morning. I saw a light in the window of Lauriston Gardens, but no one lives in that house. So I went to have a look.'

'Very good,' said Sherlock.

'I found the body in the old dining room. I needed to find another policeman to help me so I went back to the street. There was no one in the street except a very tall man. He wasn't important. He was drinking wine and I couldn't understand what he was saying, so I told him to leave! I shouted and another policeman came.'

'Where did that tall man go?' asked Sherlock.

'I don't know,' answered the policeman.

'Why not?' Sherlock asked. He left the house and didn't say goodbye to Rance.

'He's the worst policeman I know!' said Sherlock. 'That tall man was the one we want. He came back to the house to find that ring we found under Drebber when the policemen came to take him away!'

poison if you eat or drink poison, you can die   **scarlet** dark red, like blood

Later, we put a note in the London newspapers.

> *Found*
> *One ring, perhaps a woman's. If it is yours, come to 221B Baker Street between eight and nine this evening. Dr John Watson.*

Sherlock gave me a ring like the one from Lauriston Gardens and we waited.

'Perhaps the tall man will come,' I thought, 'then we can catch him. Or perhaps he will send a friend?'

***

Just after eight o'clock, someone came to our door. The person came into the house and up to our rooms. We were ready for him. But when the door opened, we didn't see a tall man, it was an old woman! She told us it was her daughter's ring. She was pleased to find it. Her daughter's husband was a difficult man and she was always worried about him. She took the ring and then she left. Sherlock ran to get his coat and went out after her.

I looked out of the window. The old woman called a taxi. Sherlock was close behind her. He got on to the back of the old woman's taxi and it left. I didn't see him again until twelve o'clock that night.

When he came back, he looked tired. 'I have something funny to tell you!' he said, and he sat down. 'Don't tell Gregson or Lestrade, but I lost that old woman.'

'How?' I asked. I couldn't understand how the great Sherlock Holmes could lose an old woman!

'She called a taxi and gave the driver her address, 13 Duncan Street. I sat on the back of her taxi until we got to Duncan Street. The driver opened the door for her, but there was no one inside! We asked at number 13, but a young family lived there, not an old woman.'

'Are you telling me that old woman left the taxi when it was travelling?' I asked.

'That wasn't an old woman,' said Sherlock. 'That was a young man who looked like an old woman. Our tall man has friends who will help him. Now Doctor, you look tired. Go to bed and get some sleep!'

I went to bed. Sherlock Holmes stayed in the living room and played his violin until late in the night. I was very tired, but I couldn't sleep. There was so much to think about.

4

AFTER-READING ACTIVITIES

Comprehension

1 Choose the right answer, A, B or C.

1 Why did Enoch Drebber die?
   - **A** ☐ He went to a house where no one lives.
   - **B** ☐ No one knows.
   - **C** ☐ No one wanted his watch or his money.

2 Why didn't Dr Watson want to go into the room?
   - **A** ☐ There were tables and chairs everywhere.
   - **B** ☐ He didn't want to see the dead man.
   - **C** ☐ Dr Watson didn't want to know how he died.

3 What did they find when the policemen took Drebber's body?
   - **A** ☐ A woman's ring.
   - **B** ☐ More blood on the floor.
   - **C** ☐ A small book with the name Joseph Stangerson inside.

4 How did Drebber die?
   - **A** ☐ The tall man wanted him to pay for something.
   - **B** ☐ His blood was on the floor.
   - **C** ☐ He died because he ate something bad.

5 Why is John Rance the worst policeman in London?
   - **A** ☐ Because he drank too much wine.
   - **B** ☐ Because Sherlock is the best policeman in London.
   - **C** ☐ Because he saw the tall man, but didn't understand who he was.

2 What do you think?

1 When Sherlock arrived at Lauriston Gardens, he looked at the road and the garden before he went into the house. Why?

   _____
   _____

2 There was a lot of blood in the room. Where did it come from?

   _____
   _____

3 Why did Drebber eat the poison?

   _____
   _____

Grammar

3 **Use the right word from the box to fill the gaps.**

> from • 's • to • why • write

'Where **(1)** _____ the taxi driver?' I asked. 'Where did the blood come **(2)** _____? Why did the man want Drebber **(3)** _____ die? **(4)** _____ did Drebber eat the poison? Why did the tall man **(5)** _____ the word RACHE?'

Writing

4 **Write about what Holmes and Watson found at Lauriston Gardens. Try to remember everything!**

> *When Holmes and Watson got to Lauriston Gardens they stayed outside the house, looking at the street and the garden. Then they...*

PRE-READING ACTIVITY

5 **Answer 'yes', 'no' or 'don't know'.**

1 Lestrade and Gregson are good policemen. _____
2 Enoch Drebber and Joseph Stangerson are friends. _____
3 Everyone in London is talking about Sherlock Holmes. _____

29

Chapter 3

The Wrong Man

▶ 6   The next day, the newspapers all talked about the 'Brixton Mystery', and I learned new things from them about Mr Drebber and Mr Stangerson.

Mr Drebber was an American. He was staying at Madame Charpentier's hotel on Torquay Terrace, near Euston Station. Staying with him was Joseph Stangerson, also American, who worked for Mr Drebber. The two men said goodbye to Mrs Charpentier on Tuesday. They wanted to catch a train from Euston Station to Liverpool. In Liverpool they had a boat to New York. Later on Tuesday night, the body of Mr Drebber was found many kilometres away in Brixton. Nobody could understand why he was in Brixton, or how he got there. Nobody knew where Stangerson was.

'It is good,' one newspaper said, 'that Mr Gregson and Mr Lestrade are working on the mystery. We are sure they will find out everything soon.' I didn't read the name of Sherlock Holmes, they only talked about Gregson and Lestrade! Those two policemen told everyone they were working on the mystery. They didn't tell anyone about asking Sherlock for help!

While I read the papers, I heard a lot of noise and lots of feet running up to our rooms. The door opened and there were six young boys, no more than about ten years old. They were very poor, with old clothes and they needed to wash.

'Who are these boys?' I asked. I wasn't happy to see them in my home!

'This is the 'Baker Street police',' Sherlock said, looking at them. They stopped talking and stood as tall as they could. 'Any news, Wiggins?' my friend asked the oldest boy.

'No, nothing,' answered Wiggins.

'Now go, and come later!'

The children ran out of the room and into the street.

'Those boys are better than ten policemen,' said Sherlock. 'Nobody sees them and they hear things that a policeman will never hear.' He took his violin and started to play a happy song.

'Are they working for you on the Brixton Mystery?' I asked.

'Yes,' he answered, 'I'm sure they'll find what I'm looking for soon. Ah, here's Gregson coming to see us,' he said, looking out of the window. 'He looks very happy about something.'

The door opened for the second time and in came Gregson.

'I have the answer to our mystery!' he said.

'His name is Arthur Charpentier, the son of Madame Charpentier who has a hotel in Camberwell.'

'Please, tell us everything. How did you find out about Madame Charpentier's?' said Sherlock.

'Ah! Mr Holmes listen to this and you will learn something,' said Gregson.

I looked at Holmes but I don't think he was really listening to Gregson.

'Inside Drebber's coat was the name of an expensive clothes shop in Bond Street. I went to the shop to ask about the American. They remembered him because they sent the coat to Madame Charpentier's hotel. And that is how I found Madame Charpentier and her son Arthur. I went to see her today. She was with her daughter, but I could see that something was wrong. The girl was very pretty, but she looked tired.

'Did you know that a man who stayed in your hotel, Mr Drebber, is dead Madame?' I asked. The mother said yes, but did not say more.

'What time did Mr Drebber leave your house to get the train at Euston?' I asked her.

'At eight o'clock,' she said. 'Mr Stangerson, the man who works for him, found out the train left at nine fifteen.'

'Did you see Mr Drebber again after he went to the station?' I asked.

'I didn't see him after he went to the station,' she said, but the daughter looked at the mother.

'We have to tell Mr Gregson about Arthur, Mother!' she said, then she ran out of the room.

'Arthur is my son,' said Madame Charpentier, 'Mr Drebber didn't die because of him, but you will think that he did. Mr Stangerson was a quiet man but Mr Drebber was not. Mr Drebber was a bad man. He drank a lot of wine, and always spoke to my daughter in a bad way. Mr Drebber came back that night because he didn't catch his train. He took my daughter, kissed her and said he wanted to

5

take her away. My daughter didn't want to be with him and then my son arrived home. He was very unhappy with Mr Drebber and took him out of the house. He didn't do it, Mr Gregson! My son is a good boy!'

'This is exciting,' Sherlock said, but he looked bored.

'I asked her some more questions about her son,' said Gregson.

'What time did your son come back after he took Drebber out of the house?'

'I don't know!,' she said. 'I waited for an hour or two, but then I went to bed and fell asleep.'

'So your son was away for two hours?'

'Yes.'

'And perhaps for four or five hours?'

'Yes,' she said.

'That was when I knew I had the right man. I found Arthur and took him to the police station,' said Gregson. 'It's funny, but Lestrade is looking for Stangerson! He's looking for the wrong man. Ah, here he is now!' he said, looking out of the window.

Lestrade was the next person in our home. He looked very worried and wasn't happy to see Gregson.

'Don't worry, Lestrade,' said Gregson, 'I've got our man! Did you find Stangerson?'

'Yes,' said Lestrade. 'I found him at Halliday's Hotel at eight this morning. He was dead.'

'So our man wasn't Arthur Charpentier!'

'Someone saw Drebber and Stangerson at Euston Station at half-past eight on Tuesday evening,' Lestrade said. 'Then we found Drebber in Brixton at two in the morning. I asked everywhere about

Stangerson, then I found out that Stangerson waited for Drebber in a hotel near the station, called Halliday's. A young boy who works at the hotel took me up to Stangerson's room, but when we got there, we saw scarlet blood running under the door.

The boy and I opened the door and found Stangerson. He was near the open window, on the floor. He was dead and cold. Someone put a long knife into his heart*. There was a lot of blood.' Lestrade stopped for a minute. 'We found another thing. Do you know what it was?' he asked. 'It was the word RACHE, written in blood,' Lestrade said.

'We have to catch that tall man,' I said. 'We don't want another dead person!'

'Did you find other things in the room?' asked Sherlock.

'There was a small box near the window, with two white pills* inside, but they aren't important.'

'You're wrong! They're the most important thing in this mystery,' said Sherlock. 'Now, please give me those pills. Watson, will you get that poor old dog from the lady at the bottom of the house?'

I got the dog. Sherlock took half of one pill and put it in a glass of milk. 'Yesterday, the lady asked me to help her old dog to die because he isn't well. I think this will work,' he said. The little dog drank the milk, but it didn't die.

Sherlock looked unhappy. 'Why isn't it dead? Why?' he asked, walking around the room. Then he said, 'I have it! I have it!'

He took half of the second pill and put it into another glass of milk. The dog drank it and died very quickly.

'You see, one pill had poison in, and the other was sugar.'

heart

pills your doctor gives you these to make you feel better

We were all looking at the dog, when the young boy Wiggins arrived.

'I have it,' Wiggins said.

Sherlock looked very happy. 'Would you ask the taxi driver to come up and carry my things,' said Sherlock.

What was Sherlock doing? I didn't know he wanted to travel. I didn't understand what was happening. Lestrade and Gregson looked at each other.

We heard a man walking up to our rooms, he opened the door and came in. He was wearing the clothes of a taxi driver and was very tall. Sherlock was near the door. When the tall man came in, Sherlock caught him. The man wanted to run away, so Lestrade, Gregson and I all ran over to help Sherlock. We all had to work hard to stop this big man.

'This is Mr Jefferson Hope,' Sherlock said, when we had the taxi driver. 'Enoch Drebber and Joseph Stangerson are dead because of this man!'

When he heard this, the man ran away from us again. He wanted to go through the window, but Sherlock and Lestrade caught him. Now he couldn't go anywhere!

'Take him to the police station at Scotland Yard,' said Sherlock. 'I'm sure he'll be happy to answer your questions!'

6

AFTER-READING ACTIVITIES

Writing

1 You work for a newspaper. Write about the Brixton Mystery. Remember to make it exciting!

Grammar

2 Make questions with these words.

1 are / boys / these / who / ?
_____

2 are / Brixton / for / Mystery / on / the / they / working / you / ?
_____

3 how / find out / about / did / you / Madame / Charpentier's / ?
_____

3 Put the verbs in the right form.

'It **(1)** _____ (*be*) good,' one newspaper **(2)** _____ (*say*), 'that Mr Gregson and Mr Lestrade **(3)** _____ (*work*) on the mystery. We are sure they **(4)** _____ (*find out*) everything soon.' I **(5)** _____ (*not read*) the name of Sherlock Holmes!

Comprehension

4 **Tick True (T) or False (F).**

                                                                                              T F

1. Mr Drebber is American but Joseph Stangerson is British. ☐ ☐
2. Mrs Charpentier doesn't like Enoch Drebber. ☐ ☐
3. Arthur Charpentier's sister wanted to go away with Drebber. ☐ ☐
4. Sherlock is interested in what Gregson is saying. ☐ ☐
5. Gregson took Arthur to the police station. ☐ ☐
6. Gregson isn't happy to see Lestrade. ☐ ☐

Speaking

5 **What did we learn about the Brixton Mystery in Chapter 3? Read the names below, then talk about your answers with a friend.**

Mr Gregson – Arthur Charpentier – Mr Lestrade – Stangerson

PRE-READING ACTIVITY

Listening

▶ 7   **6** **What do you think will be in the next chapter? Read these phrases then listen and tick the box (✓) when you hear them.**

1. The white man came to live in America. ☐
2. Nothing but sun and dry salt. ☐
3. If I die now. ☐
4. Kiss it better like Mother did. ☐

39

Chapter 4

Lucy Ferrier

▶ 7 Many years ago, when the white man came to live in America, there was a big place called the Sierra Blanco in Colorado and Utah. It was a bad place where nobody could live. It had no water, no trees, no birds or animals. There was nothing but sun and dry salt.

On May 4th, 1847, a tall man stood on a small mountain. If you saw him then, you couldn't say if he was forty or sixty years old. He was dying because he couldn't find anything to eat or drink. He was looking for water but there was no water anywhere.

'I think my time has come!' he said to himself. 'If I die now or if I die in my bed twenty years from now, it is the same thing.'

He found a place to sit. He was carrying something inside a big coat. He put it down and the thing started to cry. Out came a small face with big, brown eyes and blonde hair. It was a little girl about five years old, in a pink* dress.

'Ow, my head!' she said. 'Kiss it better like Mother did! Where's mother?'

The man kissed it. 'Mother's gone. I think you'll see her again soon.'

---

pink when you put red and white together you make pink

▶ 8   'Gone?' said the little girl in the pink dress. 'She didn't say goodbye. She's been away for three days now. Hey! There's no water here and nothing to eat!'

'No, dear girl. Do you remember we don't have any water? Mr Bender was the first to die, then Indian Pete and Mrs McGregor, then your mother.'

'So Mother is dead too?' The little girl started to cry. Then she stopped. 'Will we die soon?'

'Yes,' the man answered. The little girl looked happy again.

'Then we'll soon see Mother and she'll have water and food for us.'

Then the old man and the little girl sat together and fell asleep. Only half an hour later everything changed! Travelling over this dry place were thousands and thousands of people. Men riding horses, women carrying heavy things, children and old people and hundreds of horses.

There were twelve men on horses at the start of these people. They stopped under the mountain where the old man and the little girl slept. The men needed to find the right road past the mountain.

Then one of the young men saw something pink on the mountain. He took four other men with him to see what it was.

They found the man and the girl in the pink dress, and woke them up.

'We're with thousands of people,' the young man said. 'We're travelling together to find a place to build a new city, where we can be safe.'

'I'm John Ferrier,' the man said. 'This little girl and I were with twenty other people, but they're all dead now.'

'Is she your daughter?' asked the young man.

'No, but from today I'll call her Lucy Ferrier.'

The man helped John and Lucy come down the mountain and took them to see a man. He looked important.

'My name is Brigham Young,' said the man. 'I'm taking these people to find a new place to live. You can come with us and we will feed you, but you will live like us and do what I tell you or we will leave you here to die.'

'We don't want to die, so we'll come with you and we'll live like you,' John said.

★ ★ ★

After travelling for many weeks, they came to a river, and here they built Salt Lake City.

John worked and worked, and after twelve years he had a lot of money. Lucy was happy with John, who was like a father to her. She was eighteen now and the most beautiful young woman in Salt Lake City.

One day, John Ferrier needed something from the city. He asked Lucy to go on her horse to get it for him. On the road were thousands and thousands of cows. Lucy was good with horses but hers didn't like the cows and wanted to run away. It didn't look good for Lucy. Then she heard a man's voice next to her.

'I'm Jefferson Hope,' he said, and took Lucy's horse away from the cows.

7

'I hope you are OK. Are you John Ferrier's daughter?' the young man asked.

'I am,' said Lucy.

'Then ask him if he remembers the Jefferson Hope family of St Louis. I think my father and he were good friends when they were young.'

'You must come and tell him yourself,' Lucy Ferrier said. 'He will want to say thank you. He loves me and says he couldn't live if I died!'

The young man looked very happy. Lucy was too young to understand, but when Jefferson Hope saw her, he knew he loved her!

'I will do everything I can to make her my wife,' he said to himself. Then he took his horse and followed the cows into Salt Lake City to get water and food for them.

That evening, Jefferson Hope came to John's house. He didn't live in Salt Lake City, but he came back the next night, and the next. Soon Lucy and he were in love! Then one day, Jefferson arrived on his horse and came walking to the house with his long legs. Lucy was in front of the house.

'I have to go away to the mountains, my beautiful girl,' he said. 'But I'll be back in two months, and when I am back we will be man and wife.' Then he took Lucy and he kissed her.

★ ★ ★

It wasn't easy in Salt Lake City. Brigham Young told everyone how to live. John Ferrier wasn't happy with that, but he didn't say anything. People who didn't do what Brigham Young said often died! One day, Brigham Young came to the door.

'I hear Lucy loves a man from *outside* Salt Lake City,' he said. 'Lucy is beautiful. She will be the wife of a man from this city, not that other man. There are two men here who want her, Enoch Drebber and Joseph Stangerson. She has one month to choose. Enoch or Joseph.'

When he went, Lucy came into the room. She was crying!

'I can't be with them,' she said, 'I love Jefferson.'

'I know,' said John. 'We'll send him a message. He'll help us.'

They sent a message to Jefferson. They went to bed but in the morning they saw something very bad! On the door of the house was the number 30 written in white. What was it? 30 was the number of days until Lucy had to be the wife of Drebber or Stangerson.

The next day when John Ferrier woke up, there was the number 29 on his bed.

'They have come into my house at night!' John said. 'How did they get in? He went to look at all the doors and windows, but they were all OK.

Every day they found a new number, in the kitchen or somewhere in the house. 28, 27, 26... 3, 2, 1 but Jefferson Hope did not come!

On the last night, Lucy said goodnight to her father.

'I will never see Jefferson again,' she said. She went to bed but she didn't sleep! The man she loved was not here and tomorrow she had to marry a different man! She was very sad.

Then, John and Lucy heard a noise. They looked out of the window and saw... Jefferson!

'I have come to take you and Lucy away,' he said to John. I have horses in the mountains. Lucy took her old pink dress, John took money, food and water. They went together into the dark night and travelled from the city. On the third day, Jefferson went to find food but when he came back, John Ferrier was dead and Lucy was gone.

He went back to Salt Lake City and asked a friend about Lucy.

'I'm sorry to tell you, they found her. She's now the wife of Enoch Drebber. He doesn't love her,' said his friend, 'he only wanted her for John's money. She's very unhappy. I think she'll die soon.'

He was right. Lucy died after one month. The women in Drebber's family were sad. On the night after she died, they sat with her dead body. It was two in the morning when a man came into the house and took the ring off her finger. He kissed her face.

'I will take this ring because she had my heart, not Drebber's. They took Lucy from me and now they will die!' he said. Then he ran out into the night.

Drebber and Stangerson heard about Jefferson, so they left Salt Lake City. Jefferson followed them to another city, but they had lots of men with them so they were safe. He couldn't do anything. Then they travelled to Russia and Denmark. Jefferson followed them, but they were always together. Then he found them in London. He was the last person they ever saw!

8

AFTER-READING ACTIVITIES

Comprehension

1 Fill in the box with what you know about Lucy Ferrier, John Ferrier and Jefferson Hope.

Lucy Ferrier aged 5	Lucy Ferrier aged 18	John Ferrier	Jefferson Hope
_____ eyes	_____ in Salt Lake City	nearly died in the _____	helps Lucy with _____
_____ hair	is good with _____	forty or sixty _____	falls in love with _____
_____ face	falls in love with _____	looks after _____	helps Lucy and John _____
wears _____	doesn't want to be the wife of _____ or _____	is like a father to _____	never forgets when someone does _____ _____
is sad that _____	she has to be the wife of _____	he works hard and _____	
thinks she will see _____ again when _____	she dies after only _____	doesn't like doing what _____ wants, but doesn't _____	

48

Grammar

2 **Find the mistakes. Then correct them.**

It was easy in Salt Lake City. Brigham Young didn't tell anyone how to live. John Ferrier was happy with that, and he said everything. People who did what Brigham Young said often lived! One day, Brigham Young didn't come to the door.

_____
_____
_____
_____
_____
_____

Writing

3 **Jefferson Hope is working away from Salt Lake City. Write a letter from Jefferson to Lucy, *or* from Lucy to Jefferson.**

_____
_____
_____
_____
_____
_____

PRE-READING ACTIVITY

4 **What will you read about in the last chapter of this book?**

1. Jefferson Hope will be free to go back to America. ☐
2. Drebber said to Jefferson that he was sorry about Lucy. ☐
3. Jefferson is sorry that Drebber is dead. ☐
4. All the newspapers will talk about the great Sherlock Holmes. ☐

Chapter 5

The End of the Game

▶ 9   We took Jefferson Hope to the police station at Scotland Yard.

'I don't have much time,' he said, when we got there. 'Are you a doctor?' he asked me.

'I am,' I said.

'Then come here and listen to my heart.'

I put my hand over his heart. It was not working well and I knew it could stop soon.

'I lived for too long in the dry mountains of America,' he said. 'I've had a difficult life and it was too much for my poor heart!'

He sat down in Sherlock's chair and started to talk to us. This is what he said.

'Drebber and Stangerson had to die! Because of them the woman I loved, Lucy Ferrier, and her father, John Ferrier, are dead. I followed them for twenty years! And now I can die a happy man because I found them.'

He stopped for a minute to ask for a glass of water, which I gave to him.

'Lucy and I wanted to be together, but she had to be the wife of Enoch Drebber. She died a month later because she was so unhappy. When I found out, I wanted Drebber to die. I went to see

Lucy for the last time and I took the ring Drebber gave her off her finger: "When I see Drebber, I will show him that ring and then he will die!"

I followed Drebber and Stangerson everywhere, but they knew about me, so they were always together or had men with them to help them, but I stayed close to them. They got tired of me and went to another city in America, but after a time I found them again, then they took a boat to Russia. I followed them. They went to Denmark and I found them in Copenhagen. They were always together, Drebber and Stangerson, I had to wait. Then they came to London. They had a lot of money and I had none. I got a job as a taxi driver. "I have English clothes and my hair is long now," I thought. "They won't know me." I found them at Charpentier's Hotel, but as before, they were always together.

Then one evening I was in my taxi, when I saw Drebber and Stangerson going in to Euston Station. Some minutes later, Drebber came out but I couldn't see Stangerson. "Now I have him," I thought. He got into a taxi and I followed him to Charpentier's Hotel. Ten minutes later, he came out with a young man, who wasn't happy with him. Drebber wanted to get away from the young man. He saw my taxi and called me over. Then he got into my taxi! "I need to drink wine," he said.

He drank all night. It was one in the morning when he told me to take him to a hotel, but I knew a house where no one lived and I took him there.

Drebber drank so much wine that night that he found it difficult to walk. We went inside the old house, and then I showed him Lucy's ring.

"Now Enoch Drebber," I said to him, "who am I?"

He looked at me and knew he was a dead man! I put a knife near his head and showed him two pills. "One is sugar and the other is poison. You have to choose one," I said to him. "If you are a really bad man then you will choose the poison. You will die and I will live. Then I will go and find Stangerson and he will also die!" I had the knife, remember and I am a very tall man. Drebber could not run away from me. He took the first pill, and I took the second. I didn't have to wait long! Very soon he was on the floor and in one minute he was dead.

I waited for twenty years for this! As you know, my heart is not good. I got excited when I was with Drebber. Blood started to come out of my nose like a scarlet river. "I'll make things difficult for the police," I thought, and I wrote RACHE with my blood. Then I left the house, but I understood that I didn't have the ring. I went back to see if it was with Drebber and found a policeman there. It was good that he didn't understand who I was! Now I wanted to find Stangerson. It was Drebber who took Lucy from me, but a friend told me it was Stangerson who took the life of John Ferrier.

I heard Stangerson was at Halliday's Hotel. I waited with my taxi, but he didn't come out all day. When Drebber didn't come back to Euston Station I think Stangerson understood I was near. I found out which was his bedroom window, and it wasn't difficult to get in. He didn't want to take a pill, so I put the knife into his heart. I used *his* blood to write RACHE!

I went back to work as a taxi driver. Then a small boy told me a man at 221B Baker Street needed a taxi. And here I am!

9

Jefferson Hope stopped talking. His face was white. We didn't say anything for a few minutes. Gregson and Lestrade took him to a room and we never saw him again. When the police took his breakfast the next day, he was dead. His heart stopped that night.

How did Sherlock know about Jefferson Hope?

'When we got to Lauriston Gardens, I knew we were looking for a taxi driver,' Sherlock said. 'The taxi was outside the house for some time. I could see where the horse walked about. The taxi didn't leave so I knew that the taxi driver was with Drebber. Two men walked up the path. I looked at the path and saw where two men walked. One had big feet, so I knew he was tall. When we saw Drebber, I saw that he had small feet so I knew that big feet was the man we needed. I also understood that Drebber died because of poison. I went close to his face. I could see the poison round his mouth.

The next day, I sent a message to a policeman I know in New York. That was a big help. He told me that when Drebber was in New York he had a problem with a man called Jefferson Hope. Then Drebber left America and went to St Petersburg. So, I asked my 'Baker Street Police' to find a tall taxi driver called Jefferson Hope. Three days later we had our man!

'You have important things to teach the police!' I said to him, when he finished.

'I don't think they'll listen to me! Here, read this.'

He gave me the morning newspaper and began to play his violin.

> **Jefferson Hope is dead**
>
> *We will never know everything about the deaths of Enoch Drebber and Joseph Stangerson. The man who took the lives of these two men was Jefferson Hope. The police found him, but he died at Scotland Yard police station last night after his heart stopped. We only know that Hope followed the two men for twenty years after his love, Lucy Ferrier died. Mr Lestrade and Mr Gregson worked hard to find the right man. They're the best policemen in the country! We can all sleep safely in our beds now!*

'Your name isn't in the newspaper!' I said.

'No,' Sherlock said happily, 'the police never tell people that I help them!'

'I will,' I said. 'I'll tell everyone!'

That day, I started to write *A Study in Scarlet*. I wanted everyone to know about the great Sherlock Holmes!

AFTER-READING ACTIVITIES

Comprehension

1 Who said this?

1 'I don't have much time.' _____
2 'I need to drink wine.' _____
3 'I sent a message to a policeman in New York.' _____
4 'You have important things to teach the police!' _____

2 Answer these questions in complete sentences.

1 Why is Jefferson's heart not working well?

2 Why does Jefferson want Drebber and Stangerson to die?

3 Jefferson thinks Drebber will take the poison pill, why?

4 Why does blood come out of Jefferson's nose?

5 What does he do with the blood and why?

6 How does Stangerson die?

Grammar

3 What did Jefferson do? Use the words in the box.

> after that • end • first • now • then • tomorrow •
> twenty • when

(1) _____ I saw Drebber leave Euston Station. For the first time in **(2)** _____ years he wasn't with Stangerson. **(3)** _____ he went to Madame Charpentier's Hotel. **(4)** _____ he left, he got into my taxi. **(5)** _____ he drank a lot of wine. **(6)** _____ I had him! I gave him poison and that was the **(7)** _____ of Drebber. **(8)** _____ I will die a happy man!

Speaking

4 Answer the questions, then talk about your answers together.

1 Who is your favourite person in this book? Why?
   _____

2 Who do you not like? Why?
   _____

3 What do you think about the policemen in this book?
   _____

4 Do you feel sad for anyone in A Study in Scarlet? Why?
   _____

Writing

5 You are Doctor Watson. Write about your friend Sherlock Holmes.

_____
_____
_____
_____
_____

FOCUS ON...

A Study in Scarlet

A *Study in Scarlet* was Arthur Conan Doyle's first book about Sherlock Holmes. He wrote it in 1886 and got £25 for it (€ 35, which is about € 3000 in today's money!) In his life, Conan Doyle wrote more than 50 stories about Sherlock Holmes and Dr Watson.

Sherlock will never die!

Sherlock Holmes is now over a hundred years old, but he is still loved by people everywhere. He is so famous that some people think he was a person who lived in London and they write letters to him, which arrive at 221B Baker Street! If you go to Baker Street, you won't find 221B. Conan Doyle made a fictional address for Sherlock and Dr Watson.

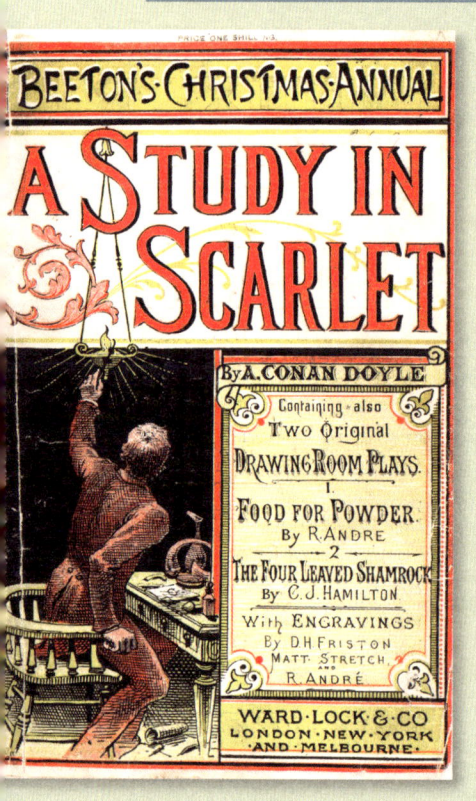

Holmes and Watson

Sherlock is a difficult person! He thinks he's better than everyone, he's always right and is sometimes cold. He doesn't get sad when someone dies, but uses his head (not his heart) to think about how, why and who. That is how he finds the answers to problems.

Dr Watson is a good person to have next to Sherlock. He asks lots of questions and is always happy to listen to Sherlock. He often thinks with his heart and not his head!

FOCUS ON...

Sir Arthur Conan Doyle

Arthur Conan Doyle was born in Edinburgh, in Scotland. His life was difficult when he was a child. His father was not well and spent the family's money. Arthur's uncles paid for him to go to a good school and then to university in Edinburgh. Do you know what he studied? Medicine! Conan Doyle was a doctor like John Watson. Conan Doyle had a teacher when he was at university, called Joseph Bell, who liked asking questions and understanding problems. He was a lot like Sherlock Holmes!

'I don't like Sherlock!'

Arthur Conan Doyle wrote about Sherlock and Dr Watson for some years, then he decided he was bored! He didn't like Sherlock. He wanted to write other books, and Sherlock took all his time. When someone wanted new Sherlock books, Conan Doyle asked them for a lot of money. 'It's too much money,' he thought, 'they will never say yes.' Of course they said yes. After that, Conan Doyle was the richest writer in England!

Bored, bored, bored

Sherlock Holmes thinks very fast and often gets bored. 'My head is like a fast car,' he says, 'give me work, give me problems, give me a difficult mystery and I am happy.'

FOCUS ON...

The Sherlock Holmes Museum

This museum in Baker Street, London, is all about the great Sherlock Holmes. The house is full of things from the 1880s, when Holmes and Watson lived in London. It's a very nice house, full of lovely chairs and tables, Dr Watson's books and even a dining room ready for lunch! When you go there, it is difficult to remember that Holmes and Watson are not real people, they're from a book!

Sherlock Holmes says

'A lot of people look, but if you want to find answers you have to see. Looking is not the same as seeing.'

'I need to use my head in my job. I cannot live a good life if I don't have to think.'

'You cannot think well with your heart, you have to use your head.'

'It is the little things that are always the most important.'

'There is nothing new under the sun. It has all been done before.'

'I hear of Sherlock everywhere!'

This is what Sherlock's brother, Mycroft, says in a Sherlock Holmes book. Sherlock Holmes is now in the cinema, on the TV and there are also Sherlock books by new writers.

FOCUS ON...

Sherlock

In 2010, the BBC asked Mark Gatiss and Steven Moffat to put Sherlock Holmes and Doctor Watson in today's London. Gatiss and Moffat are big fans of Sherlock Holmes and loved reading about him when they were young. They were happy to write a new TV programme about Sherlock! Sherlock is Benedict Cumberbatch and Dr Watson is Martin Freeman. People in more than 200 countries watch the BBC's *Sherlock*. It's important to be like Sherlock when you see *Sherlock*. You have to *watch* and not only look, because it is very fast!

Benedict Cumberbatch

Sherlock in Hollywood

Two Hollywood films were also made from Conan Doyle's books. Here, Sherlock is Robert Downey Junior, Dr Watson is Jude Law and we are in London in the 1880s. Of course, it's Moriarty who is Sherlock's biggest problem!

Robert Downey Junior and Jude Law

Benedict Cumberbatch says...

People love the new Sherlock because he's different from most people. He works hard and never forgets important things. I'd like to remember things as well as Sherlock!

Task
When did Conan Doyle write the first Sherlock book?
_____
What was the name of Conan Doyle's university teacher?
_____
Conan Doyle was a writer, but what was his second job?
_____

TEST YOURSELF

'It's the little things that are important.' Are you as good as Sherlock? Answer these questions to find out!

1. What time does Sherlock go to bed?
   - **A** ☐ Late, he likes to play his violin all night.
   - **B** ☐ He doesn't sleep much.
   - **C** ☐ Before ten – he likes to be up early.

2. What was on Drebber's business cards?
   - **A** ☐ Enoch J. Drebber, Cleveland, Ohio.
   - **B** ☐ Enoch J. Drebber, New York, USA.
   - **C** ☐ Enoch J. Drebber, Sierra Blanco, Colorado.

3. What was the name of Sherlock's young 'policeman'?
   - **A** ☐ Gregson
   - **B** ☐ Wiggins
   - **C** ☐ Rance

4. Where and at what time did Lestrade find Stangerson?
   - **A** ☐ At Euston Station at two in the morning.
   - **B** ☐ At Charpentier's Hotel on Tuesday evening.
   - **C** ☐ At Halliday's hotel at eight in the morning.

5. What was the name of the city that Brigham Young built?
   - **A** ☐ Cleveland
   - **B** ☐ Salt Lake City
   - **C** ☐ Utah

6. Where did Drebber go after he left New York?
   - **A** ☐ Russia
   - **B** ☐ England
   - **C** ☐ France

SYLLABUS

Level A1

Syllabus
Nouns
Plural
Possessive 's

Pronouns
Indefinite: *some-, no-, any-, every-* (*body/thing*)
Subject and object

Determiners
Ordinal numbers: *first – hundredth*
Quantifiers *some/any, more,*
Distributives: *another, other, each*

Adjectives
Comparative: *er/more* + adjective...*than, as....as*
Superlative: *the -est* (*in/of*), *most* + adjective

Verb forms and tenses
Negative questions
Present Continuous
Present Simple
Past Simple of listed irregular verbs
will for offers, requests and with future meaning
can
could for past ability and possibility
have to for obligation
Common phrasal verbs with transparent meanings

Adverbs
Adverbs of frequency
Comparative: *as....as*
Indefinite: *somewhere, nowhere, anywhere, everywhere*
Question words

Sentence types
Two clauses joined with *so, before, after, when*
know, think, hope etc + *that* clause

YOUNG ADULT ELI READERS

STAGE 1
Jonathan Swift, *Gulliver's Travels*
Sir Arthur Conan Doyle, *The Hound of the Baskervilles*
Daniel Defoe, *Robinson Crusoe*
Sir Arthur Conan Doyle, *A Study in Scarlet*

STAGE 2
Charles Dickens, *Great Expectations*
William Shakespeare, *Romeo and Juliet*
Bram Stoker, *Dracula*
William Shakespeare, *A Midsummer Night's Dream*
Robert Louis Stevenson, *The Strange Case of Dr Jekyll and Mr Hyde*
Jerome K. Jerome, *Three Men in a Boat*
William Shakespeare, *Hamlet*

STAGE 3
Charlotte Brontë, *Jane Eyre*
Jane Austen, *Pride and Prejudice*
Oscar Wilde, *The Picture of Dorian Gray*
William Shakespeare, *Macbeth*
Jane Austen, *Sense and Sensibility*
Edith Wharton, *The Age of Innocence*
Wikie Collins, *The Woman in White*
Henry James, *The portrait of a Lady*

STAGE 4
James Joyce, *Dubliners*
Mary Shelley, *Frankenstein*
Henry James, *The Turn of the Screw*
Emily Brontë, *Wuthering Heights*
Edgar Allan Poe, *Stories of Mystery and Suspense*
Charles and Mary Lamb, *Tales from Shakespeare*
Charles Dickens, *A Tale of Two Cities*
Anthony Hope, *The Prisoner of Zenda*
Hermann Melville, *Moby Dick*

STAGE 5
Virginia Woolf, *Mrs Dalloway*
Francis Scott Fitzgerald, *The Great Gatsby*
William Makepeace Thackeray, *Vanity Fair*

STAGE 6
Joseph Conrad, *Heart of Darkness*
J. Borsbey & R. Swan, Editors, *A Collection of First World War Poetry*
Oscar Wilde, *The Importance of Being Earnest*

YOUNG ADULT ELI READERS LIGHT

Edgar Allan Poe, *The Narrative of Arthur Gordon Pym of Nantucket*

Natsume Sōseki, *Botchan*